MEDICAL MOBILIZATION
THEN AND NOW

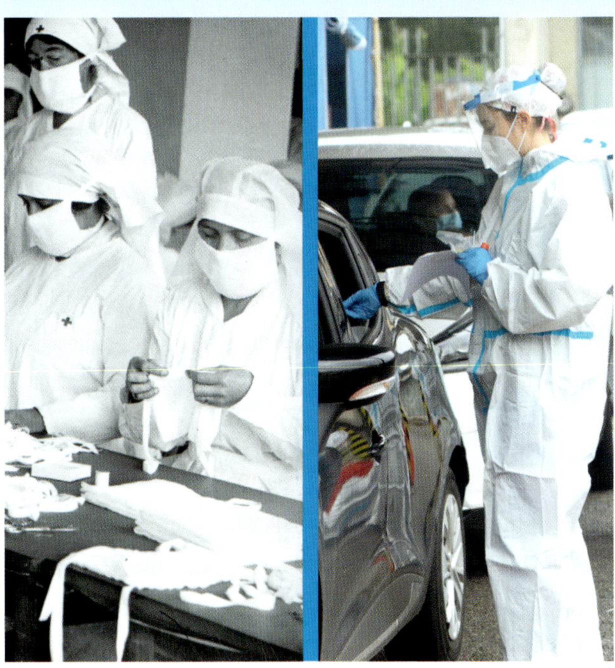

Abdo & Daughters
MIDDLE GRADE NONFICTION

An imprint of Abdo Publishing
abdobooks.com

Elsie Olson

ABDOBOOKS.COM

Published by Abdo Publishing, a division of ABDO, PO Box 398166, Minneapolis, Minnesota 55439. Copyright © 2022 by Abdo Consulting Group, Inc. International copyrights reserved in all countries. No part of this book may be reproduced in any form without written permission from the publisher. Abdo & Daughters™ is a trademark and logo of Abdo Publishing.

Printed in the United States of America, North Mankato, Minnesota

052021

092021

Design: Kelly Doudna, Mighty Media, Inc.

Production: Mighty Media, Inc.

Editor: Jessica Rusick

Cover Photographs: National Archives and Records Administration (left); Shutterstock Images

Interior Photographs: CDC, pp. 22–23; Jae C. Hong/AP Images, p. 41; Keystone Press/Alamy, pp. 26–27; Library of Congress, p. 15; Mario Tama/Getty Images, p. 39; Mark Lennihan/AP Images, p. 43 (top); NARA/Wikimedia Commons, p. 25; Nathan Denette/AP Images, pp. 34–35; National Archives and Records Administration, pp. 1 (left), 8–9, 10, 16, 17, 18, 20, 21; National Library of Medicine, pp. 12–13, 45; Navy Medicine/Flickr, pp. 14, 29, 37; Ng Han Guan/AP Images, p. 6; NIH/Flickr, pp. 43, 44; Shutterstock Images, pp. 1, 4–5, 7, 11, 24 (bottom), 30, 31 (both), 32, 38, 42; Strategic National Stockpile Communications Team, p. 24; The White House/Flickr, pp. 33, 36

Design Elements: Shutterstock Images

LIBRARY OF CONGRESS CONTROL NUMBER: 2020949732

PUBLISHER'S CATALOGING-IN-PUBLICATION DATA

Names: Olson, Elsie, author.

Title: Medical mobilization: then and now / by Elsie Olson

Other title: then and now

Description: Minneapolis, Minnesota : Abdo Publishing, 2022 | Series: Pandemics | Includes online resources and index

Identifiers: ISBN 9781532195600 (lib. bdg.) | ISBN 9781098216337 (ebook)

Subjects: LCSH: Medical care--Juvenile literature. | Medical protocols--Juvenile literature. | Medical screening--Juvenile literature. | Epidemics--History--Juvenile literature. | Diseases and history--Juvenile literature. | Medical archaeology--Juvenile literature

Classification: DDC 614.5--dc23

TABLE OF CONTENTS

Belgian funeral home workers prepare a COVID-19 victim's body. Belgium had one of the worst COVID-19 death rates in the world.

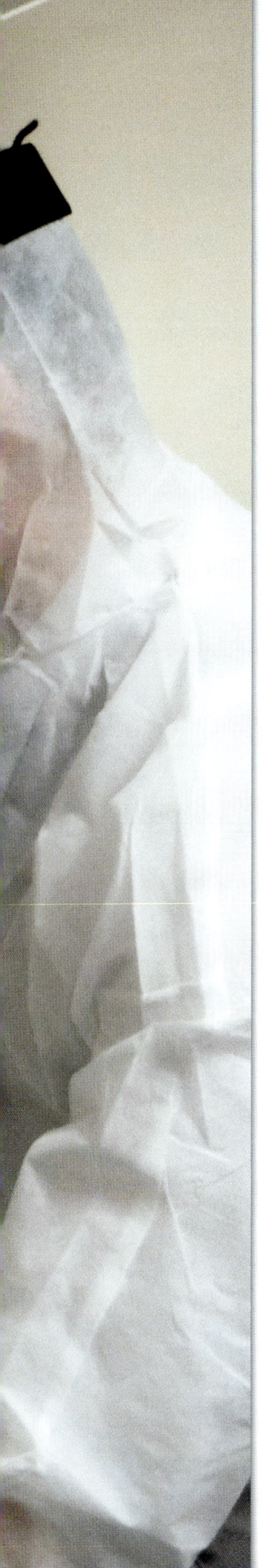

Chapter 1

PANDEMICS THEN AND NOW

Every year, billions of people fall ill with infectious diseases caused by viruses. In late 2019, a new virus emerged in Wuhan, China. The virus was a strain of coronavirus called SARS-CoV-2. It caused a disease that scientists named COVID-19.

Coronaviruses commonly cause sickness in animals. But sometimes they mutate, or change, to infect humans. Coronaviruses cause upper respiratory infections in people. These infections are typically mild. However, COVID-19 was not caused by a typical coronavirus. As COVID-19 spread, health officials realized that SARS-CoV-2 was more contagious and deadly than most other coronaviruses.

A Pandemic Begins

Epidemiologists, doctors, nurses, and scientists worked frantically to understand and contain COVID-19. However, by early 2020, it had

In January 2021, a team of WHO experts traveled to Wuhan to study COVID-19's origins.

spread to hundreds of countries. On March 11, the World Health Organization (WHO) declared COVID-19 a pandemic. A pandemic occurs when a disease spreads throughout the world. During a pandemic, new infections occur at the same time in many different places.

Declaring a pandemic allowed public health experts to use emergency resources to respond to the virus. It also highlighted that COVID-19 was a global problem. Beating the disease would require cooperation from health experts around the world.

Difficult Work

Doctors and nurses worked tirelessly to care for sick COVID-19 patients. But the virus was challenging to treat. Patients experienced a wide range of symptoms, and doctors experimented with many different treatments.

The stress of the pandemic took a physical and emotional toll on the health-care heroes who fought the virus. In many places, there were not enough doctors and nurses to care for patients. Frontline health workers were overworked and exhausted. Many became sick with COVID-19 themselves. Meanwhile, epidemiologists and drug companies raced to develop COVID-19 treatments and vaccines.

COVID-19 was not the first pandemic to test the world's medical professionals. Just over 100 years earlier, the world had been ravaged by an influenza virus. The 1918 influenza pandemic was the deadliest in modern history.

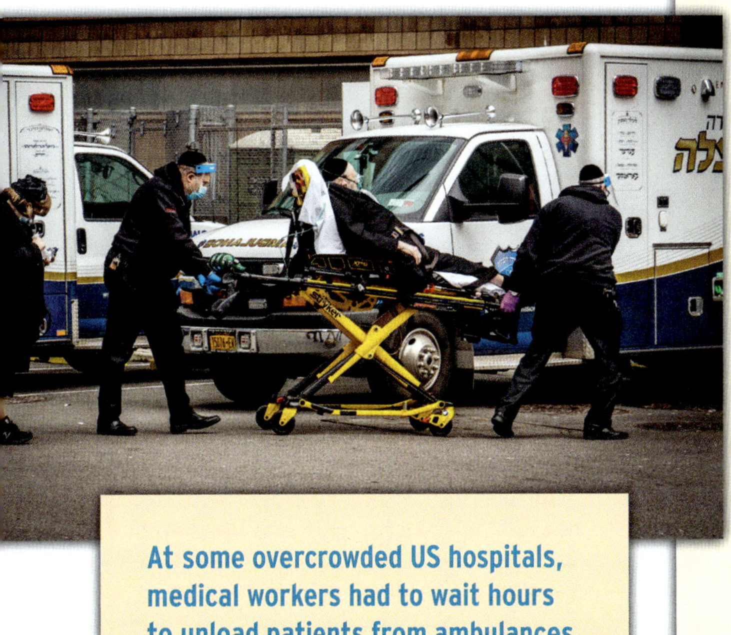

PANDEMICS BY THE NUMBERS

Coronaviruses cause 15 to 30 percent of common colds. But since 2000, three strains of coronavirus have caused more serious, widespread outbreaks of disease.

SEVERE ACUTE RESPIRATORY SYNDROME

Nickname: SARS

Year discovered: 2003

Known infections: 8,098

Deaths: 774

Case fatality rate: 9.6%

MIDDLE EAST RESPIRATORY SYNDROME

Nickname: MERS

Year discovered: 2012

Known infections: 2,519

Deaths: 866

Case fatality rate: 35%

CORONAVIRUS DISEASE 2019

Nickname: COVID-19

Year discovered: 2019

Known infections: more than 129 million by April 2021

Deaths: more than 2.8 million by April 2021

Case fatality rate: 2%

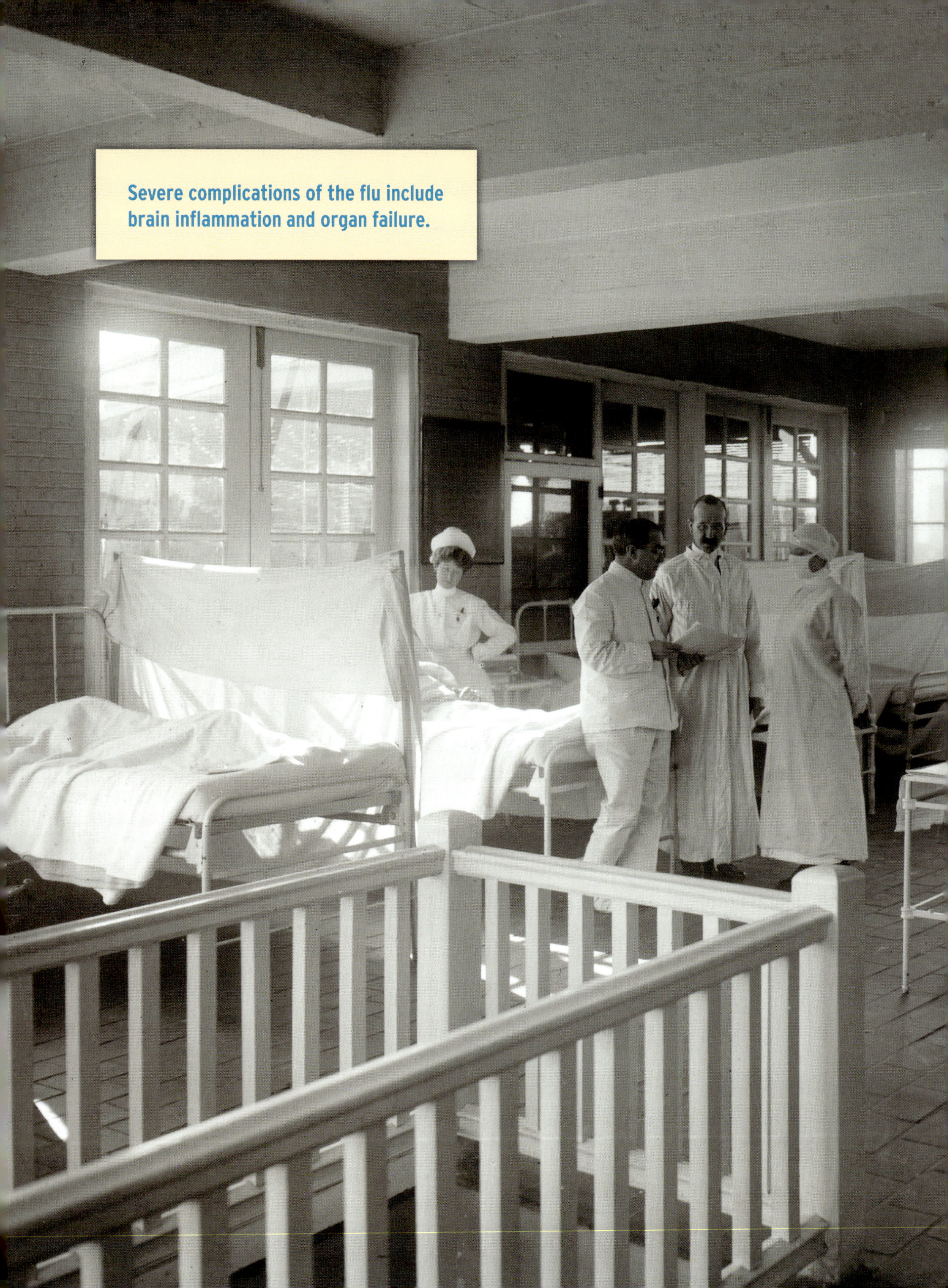
Severe complications of the flu include
brain inflammation and organ failure.

Chapter 2

INFLUENZA ATTACKS

Influenza, or the flu, is a viral upper respiratory disease. Influenza typically affects people during fall and winter. This yearly period is known as flu season.

During a typical flu season, the flu infects between 9 million and 45 million Americans, killing between 12,000 and 61,000. Influenza is usually most severe in people with weak immune systems. This includes the very old, the very young, and people with certain health conditions.

An Unusual Virus

Historians aren't sure where the 1918 influenza virus originated. But the first documented case occurred at Camp Funston, a US Army camp in Kansas, in March 1918. More than 1,000 of the camp's 54,000 soldiers became ill with the virus, and 38 soldiers died from it.

The 1918 pandemic began during a turbulent time in world history. Throughout the spring of 1918, the US military sent more than 100,000 troops around the world to fight in World War I. The troops carried the deadly virus with them overseas.

Influenza viruses spread through airborne droplets produced when a person talks, breathes, coughs, or sneezes. The tightly packed military ships, trenches, and battlefields of World War I helped the virus spread quickly among soldiers. Soon, the virus spread from soldiers to civilians around the world.

Three Waves

The 1918 pandemic struck in three waves. Infections peaked during each wave and subsided between waves. The first wave began in spring 1918 and dropped off in the summer.

A mutated version of the virus caused a second wave in the fall of 1918. After an influenza virus enters a person's body, it invades cells and uses them to make copies of itself. Like all viruses, influenza can mutate as it makes copies. Mutations in the 1918 virus caused it to become deadlier and more contagious.

The second wave subsided by the end of 1918. A third and final wave began in January 1919 and ended in the summer. The pandemic was over. But its effects on patients and health workers had been devastating.

PANDEMICS BY THE NUMBERS

The 1918 pandemic was caused by a virus called H1N1 Influenza A. The disease was nicknamed the Spanish flu because many people mistakenly believed the virus came from Spain.

H1N1 INFLUENZA A

Nickname: Spanish flu
Year discovered: 1918
Estimated infections: more than 500 million
Estimated deaths: more than 50 million
Case fatality rate: 2.5%

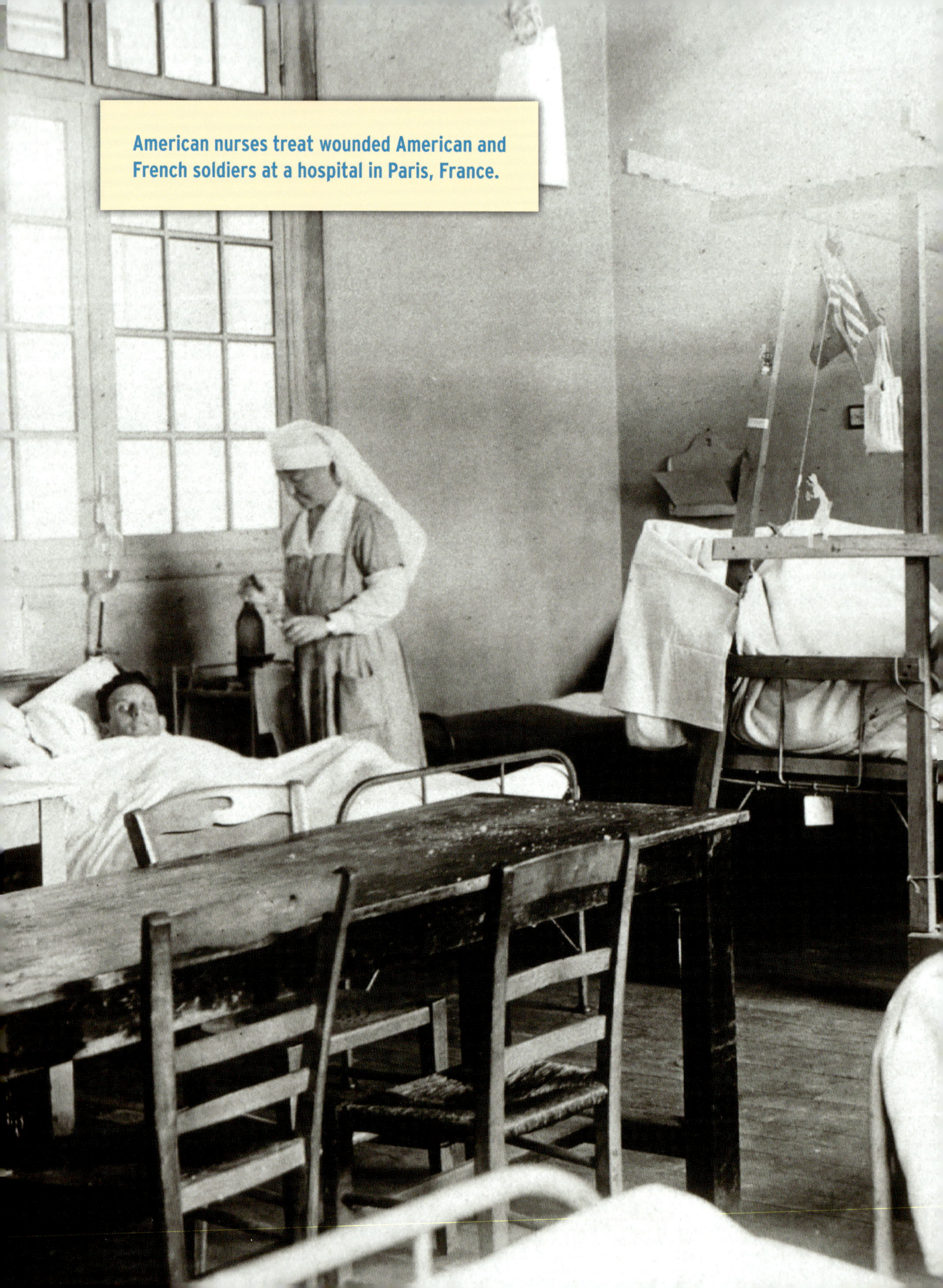

American nurses treat wounded American and
French soldiers at a hospital in Paris, France.

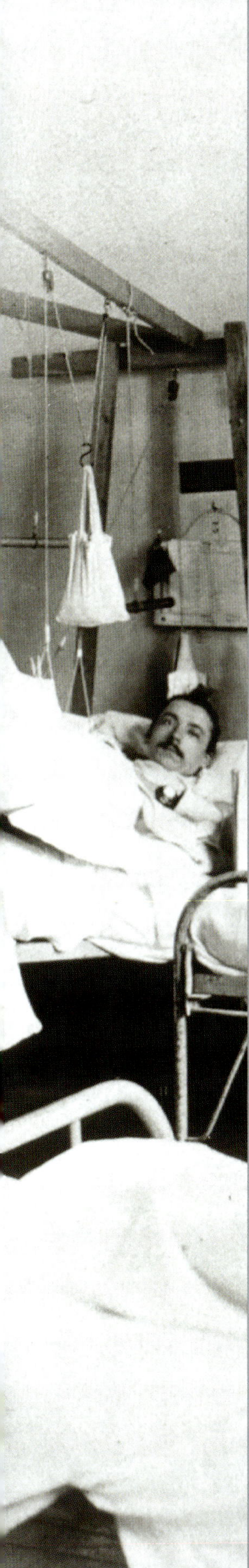

Chapter 3

A CRISIS LIKE NO OTHER

In 1918, World War I had already put a strain on health workers. Many American doctors and nurses traveled with US soldiers to battlefields. This left a shortage of medical professionals back home. The 1918 pandemic further overwhelmed doctors and nurses.

Like SARS-CoV-2, the influenza virus was much deadlier and more contagious than a typical virus of its kind. It also affected an unexpected population. In addition to being deadly in those with weak immune systems, the 1918 influenza virus was unusually deadly for healthy adults between the ages of 20 and 40. In severe cases, the flu could cause pneumonia, a bacterial infection that inflames the lungs. Antibiotics, which today's doctors use to treat pneumonia, would not be discovered for another decade. So, many flu victims died from these secondary infections.

Doctors in 1918 were unprepared to treat this deadly influenza. At the time, viral science was new. Scientists knew that viruses caused some diseases in humans. However, they did not know that influenza was caused by a virus. Most doctors treating flu patients thought the infections were caused by bacteria.

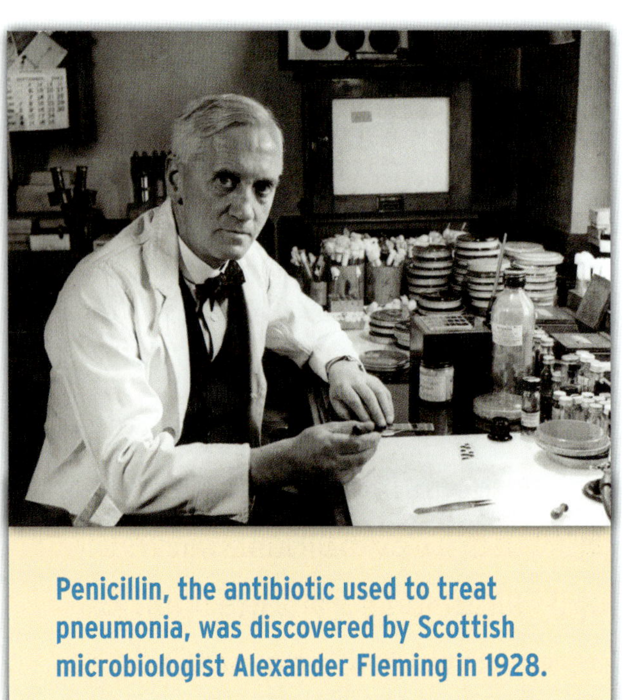

Penicillin, the antibiotic used to treat pneumonia, was discovered by Scottish microbiologist Alexander Fleming in 1928.

Treatment

With limited medical knowledge, doctors had few ways to treat influenza patients. Many doctors experimented with common treatments used to treat other diseases. These treatments included quinine, a medicine used to treat malaria. Other treatments included herbs and essential oils. However, these methods did little to help influenza patients.

Doctors also focused on treating patients' symptoms. Influenza symptoms included fever, body aches, and coughing. Doctors encouraged patients to rest and drink lots of fluid. A mixture of cinnamon and milk was given to reduce fever. Patients also took pain-relieving medications such as aspirin.

Health experts knew that germs spread easily in poorly ventilated areas. So, doctors at many hospitals opened windows or treated patients outdoors to improve ventilation. At Walter Reed Hospital in Maryland, an influenza ward was set up on a screened porch. At Camp Brooks Hospital in Boston, Massachusetts, flu patients were housed in large tents. During the day, the tents were opened to expose patients to fresh air and sunlight. Fewer patients died at this hospital than in many other hospitals.

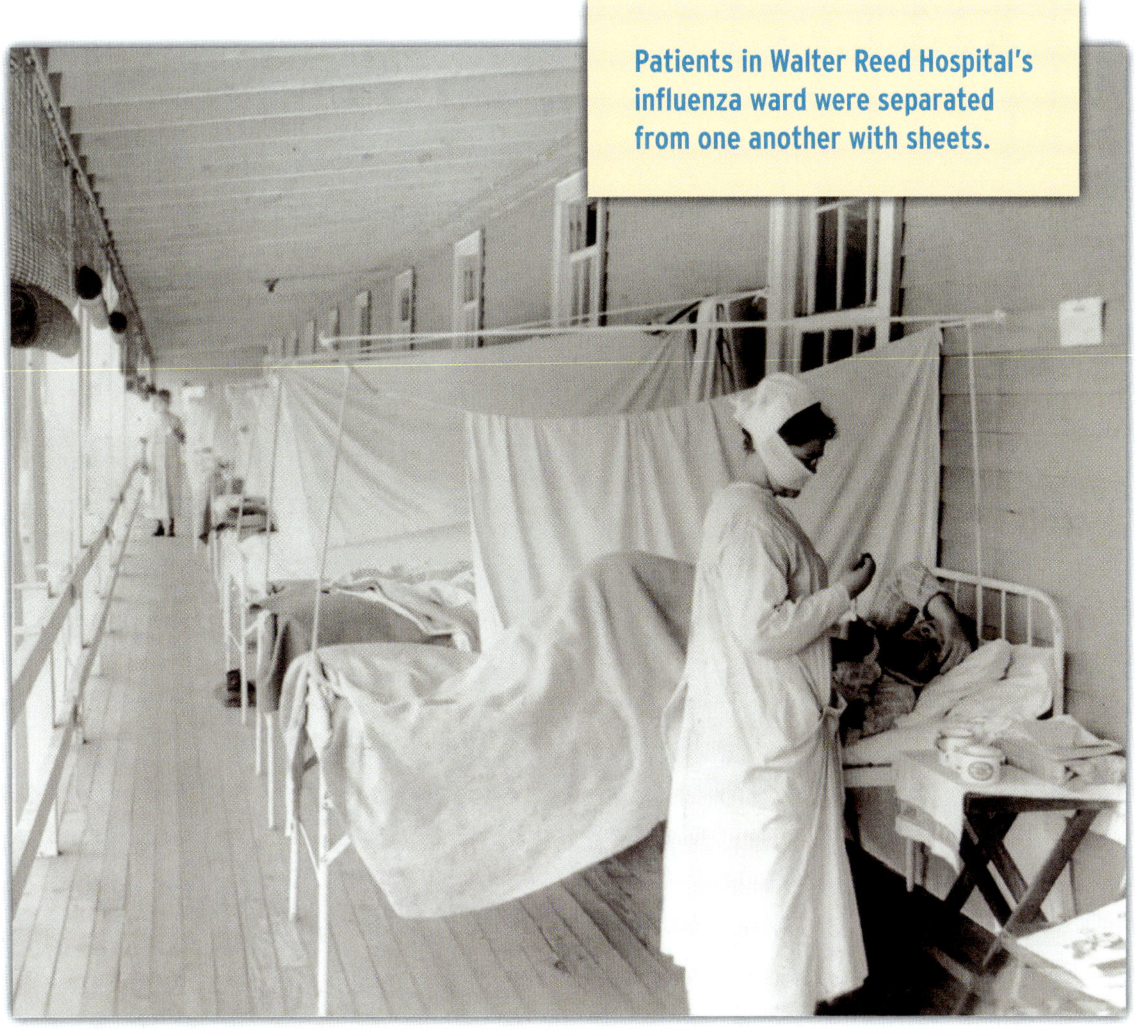

Patients in Walter Reed Hospital's influenza ward were separated from one another with sheets.

In 1918, there were no vaccines or antiviral medications to help prevent or reduce the severity of flu infections. Today, the US government encourages all Americans to receive a flu shot every flu season to reduce their risk of getting the flu. Antiviral medications, such as Tamiflu, can be given to patients suffering from influenza. These drugs can reduce the length and severity of a flu infection.

Nurses at Work

As influenza cases rose, it became impossible for doctors to treat every influenza patient. As a result, the care for most flu patients fell to nurses. They worked long hours to keep patients fed and hydrated. They changed bedding and administered pain-relieving medication.

Many hospitals became overfilled with influenza patients during the pandemic's second wave. So, nurses traveled to care for people in their homes. There, in addition to providing medical care, nurses often made meals and cared for children.

A nurse gathers water for patients at an outdoor influenza hospital in Brookline, Massachusetts.

Amid the pandemic's second wave, US nurses faced supply shortages. Fresh bedding and pain medicines were difficult to obtain. The country also faced a serious nursing shortage. In Philadelphia, Pennsylvania, a single nurse saw as many as 40 patients in a day. Some patients died while waiting for medical treatment.

Nursing students went to hospitals to help with the shortages. The American Red Cross (ARC) also trained volunteers as nurses. The ARC is a national charity with a history of providing disaster relief in the United States. Despite the ARC's efforts, nursing volunteers were often inexperienced. They could not provide the same quality of care as professional nurses.

Dangers and Precautions

Doctors and nurses risked their lives caring for flu patients. Some contracted influenza themselves. Others had to take care of colleagues or family members who had fallen ill.

At many hospitals, medical workers took precautions to protect themselves and their patients. Doctors and nurses regularly wore masks, head coverings, and medical gowns while treating patients. This personal protective equipment (PPE) was frequently changed so it remained clean. Hospital rooms and bedsheets were also disinfected between patients. And, doctors and nurses also regularly sanitized their hands to kill germs.

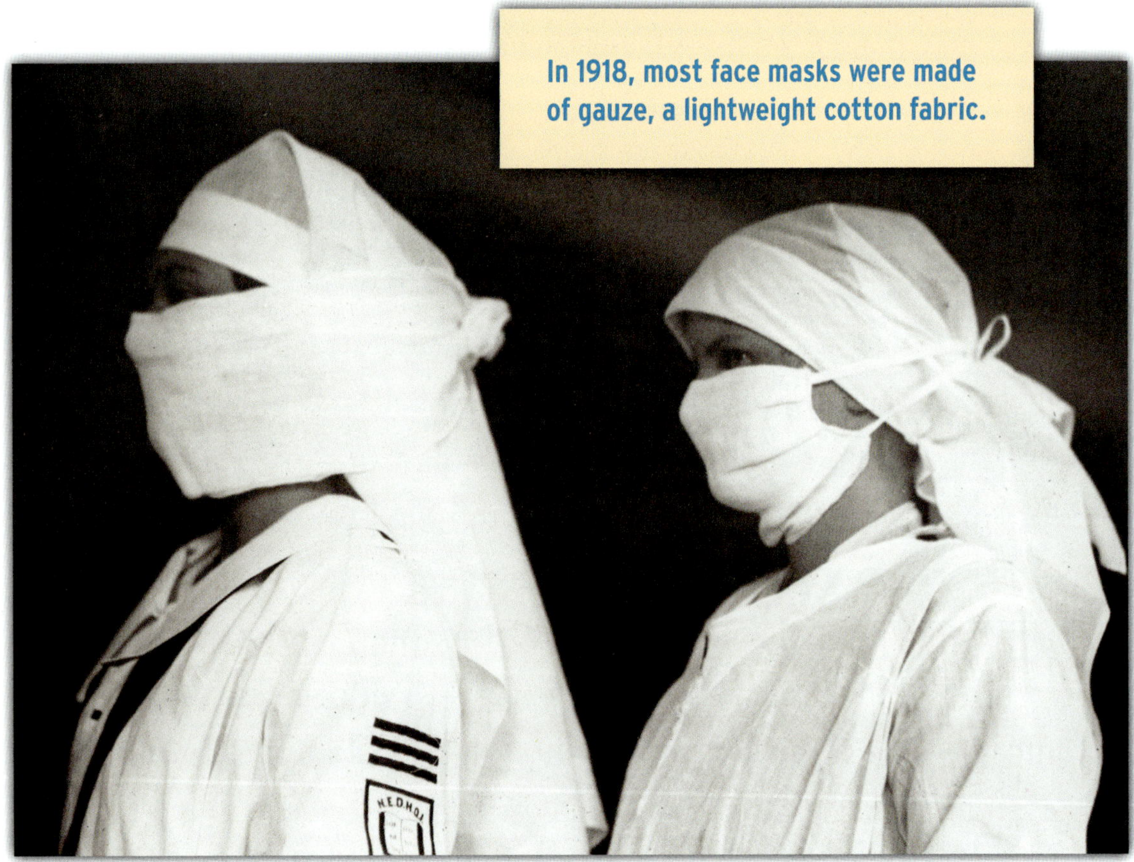

In 1918, most face masks were made of gauze, a lightweight cotton fabric.

Public Health Response

Public health officials also responded to the pandemic. At the time, public health was largely the concern of individual cities and states instead of the federal government. So, communities took different approaches to fighting the virus. Many communities tried to slow the spread of the virus as much as possible. Health officials recommended that people frequently wash their hands and disinfect surfaces to kill germs. Officials also recommended that people wear face masks to contain respiratory droplets that could spread influenza.

In some cities, people were encouraged to sleep with their windows open to improve ventilation. Crowded public places such as schools, theaters, and churches closed. Large social gatherings were discouraged. In Kansas City, Missouri, no more than 20 people were allowed at weddings and funerals. In New York City, factory workers were ordered to work staggered shifts. This reduced crowding on the city's busy subway system, which many workers used to get to and from work.

THEN VS. TODAY

The 1918 pandemic encouraged many new hygiene practices that are common today. These include frequent handwashing, covering one's mouth when coughing and sneezing, and sanitizing public areas.

A barbershop in California gives haircuts outdoors to avoid overcrowding inside.

Different Responses

Many pandemic safety measures were unpopular. So, some cities were slow to adopt them. This meant different cities were affected by the pandemic differently. Officials in St. Louis, Missouri, adopted safety measures soon after it became clear that influenza was spreading there. In other cities, such as Philadelphia, officials waited longer to adopt precautions. At the height of the pandemic, St. Louis had a death rate of 358 per 100,000 people. Meanwhile, Philadelphia was one of the hardest-hit cities in the country. It had a death rate of 748 per 100,000 people.

By the summer of 1919, the third and final wave of the pandemic had subsided. Health officials estimate the 1918 pandemic infected up to 500 million people. This was one-third of the world's population. The virus killed as many as 50 million people, including 675,000 in the United States. The 1918 pandemic would not be the last pandemic the world faced. But it would change the way health workers and public health officials responded to future health crises.

Dr. Thomas Tuttle was the health commissioner of Washington State. He oversaw the state's health department. During the 1918 pandemic, Tuttle worked with local leaders to coordinate a pandemic response. He pushed leaders to encourage wearing masks and to ban public gatherings. Tuttle's strategies worked. Washington's infection rate stayed low for the six weeks the restrictions were in place. But infections increased once they were removed.

Police officers in Seattle wear masks during the second wave of the 1918 pandemic.

The CDC was originally founded to combat malaria in the United States. Malaria is a disease carried by mosquitoes.

Chapter 4

HEALTH CARE EVOLVES

After the 1918 pandemic, the US government began implementing a federal health strategy. In 1946, the Centers for Disease Control and Prevention (CDC) was founded in Atlanta, Georgia. It focuses on preventing contagious diseases in the United States.

In 1948, the United States joined nations around the world to launch the World Health Organization. It is dedicated to coordinating global health care. In 1953, several existing US health agencies combined to form what would later be called the Department of Health and Human Services (HHS). This cabinet department works closely with the CDC to provide national health recommendations. During future public health emergencies, the HHS and CDC worked with the ARC to send nurses and doctors to hard-hit areas.

In 1999, Congress directed the CDC and HHS to set up a stockpile of medicines and vaccines

In 2017, the SNS sent medical supplies and personnel to Puerto Rico to help in the aftermath of Hurricane Maria.

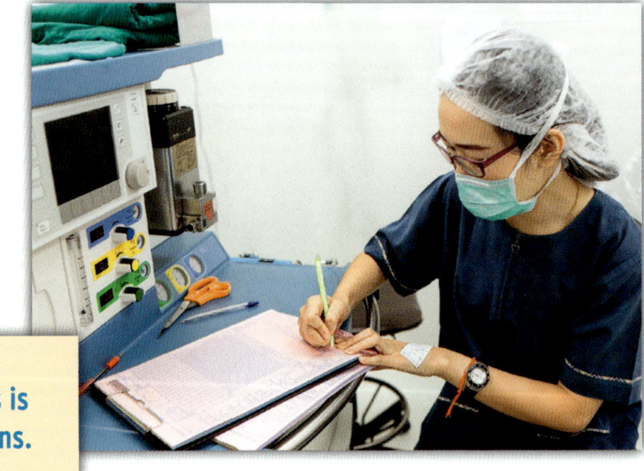

that could be given to states during future health emergencies. In 2003, this became the Strategic National Stockpile (SNS). The SNS was later expanded to include face masks and medical devices. Officials hoped the SNS would help prevent the supply shortages that had occurred during the 1918 pandemic.

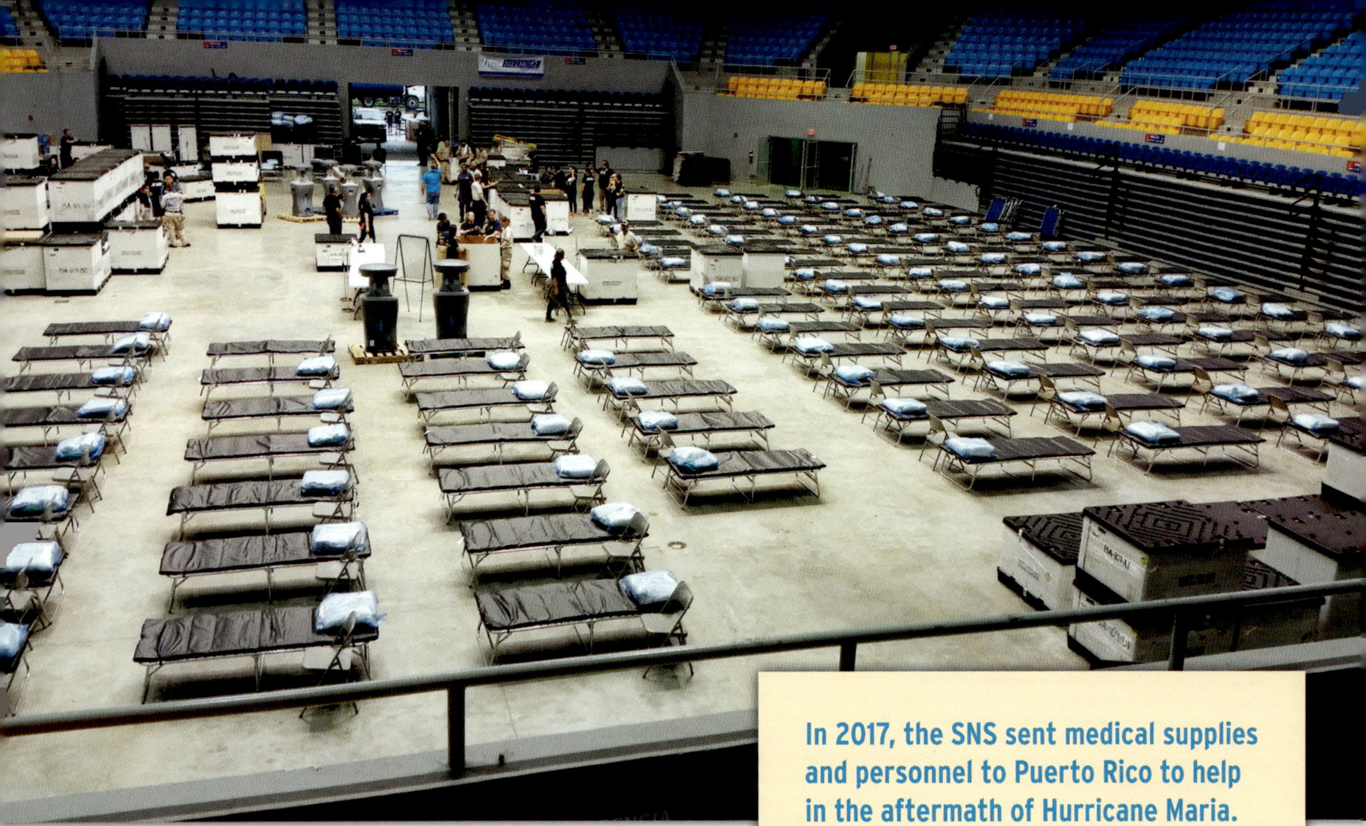

Changes in Nursing

The 1918 pandemic also changed the nursing profession. Many people

One of an LPN's typical duties is recording a patient's vital signs.

had previously viewed nurses as assistants to doctors. However, the pandemic proved that nurses could care for patients and make decisions without a doctor's supervision.

The pandemic also showed the danger of nursing shortages. In 1943, the US government began helping student nurses pay for school. This ensured more people could complete nursing programs. Nursing schools also began training nursing assistants, known as licensed practical nurses (LPNs). LPNs could be trained in less than a year, unlike the two to three years of school required to be a registered nurse (RN). LPNs could then work as nurses under the supervision of an RN.

In 1918, much of the United States was segregated. Medical care was no exception. Black nurses were banned from working for the ARC and many hospitals. However, the nursing shortage in 1918 encouraged medical professionals to rethink these racist policies. That year, the first Black nurses joined the ARC. Today, Black nurses make up nearly 10 percent of US nurses.

In 1941, Della H. Raney became the first Black nurse accepted into the US Army.

American scientist Jonas Salk helped
develop the first influenza vaccine.

Chapter 5

THE COVID-19 PANDEMIC

In the century after the 1918 pandemic, science and medicine made incredible strides. The first antibiotics were discovered in the 1920s. These could cure bacterial infections. The first influenza vaccine was approved for use in the 1940s. It could reduce a person's chances of getting the flu by as much as 60 percent. Antiviral drugs were developed in the 1960s. These could reduce the severity of a viral infection.

Thanks to these and other medical breakthroughs, deaths from infectious diseases dropped by more than 90 percent from 1900 to 1999. While there were other outbreaks, epidemics, and pandemics, none approached the severity of the 1918 flu pandemic. Nonetheless, viruses continued to spread and mutate. Epidemiologists warned the next great pandemic was inevitable.

The Next Great Pandemic

COVID-19 was first detected in Wuhan, China, in December 2019. Doctors there treated several patients suffering from the then unknown illness. The patients experienced fevers, difficulty breathing, and lung damage. WHO epidemiologists were concerned by the outbreak. However, Chinese authorities assured them the disease did not seem overly contagious. Chinese scientists studied the virus while the WHO monitored it.

Meanwhile, COVID-19 spread within China. Hospitals in Wuhan were soon overrun with COVID-19 patients. On January 13, 2020, the first case outside of China was recorded, in Thailand. The United States documented its first case on January 20. By March, the virus had spread to hundreds of countries.

A Mysterious Infection

Epidemiologists around the world struggled to understand the novel coronavirus. Infected people reported a long list of symptoms. Some symptoms were commonly associated with coronavirus infections. These included a cough, runny nose, and sore throat. But other symptoms were unusual. These included loss of taste or smell, nausea, and diarrhea.

Some people who caught the virus had no symptoms. Others experienced very mild symptoms. But for some people, COVID-19 was life threatening. People with severe symptoms experienced trouble breathing and organ failure.

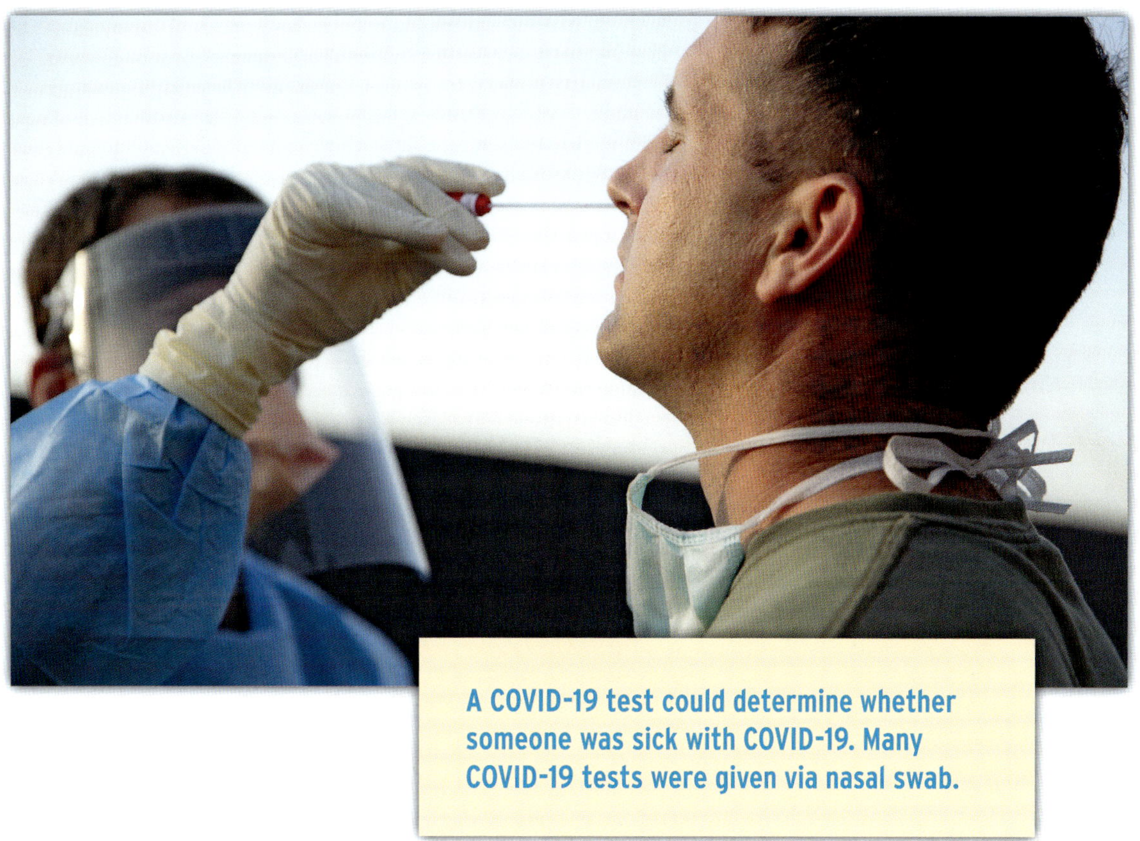

A COVID-19 test could determine whether someone was sick with COVID-19. Many COVID-19 tests were given via nasal swab.

Symptoms could go from mild to severe in a matter of hours. Some people with the disease appeared to recover at home before becoming so ill they had to be hospitalized. The coronavirus was particularly deadly for people over the age of 65. It was also deadly for those with health issues such as high blood pressure. However, even young, healthy people could become very ill. Epidemiologists were unsure why some people became so much sicker than others.

Overwhelming the System

As COVID-19 cases increased in spring 2020, many hospitals around the world faced space, equipment, and health-worker shortages. One particularly hard-hit country was Italy. The country reported its

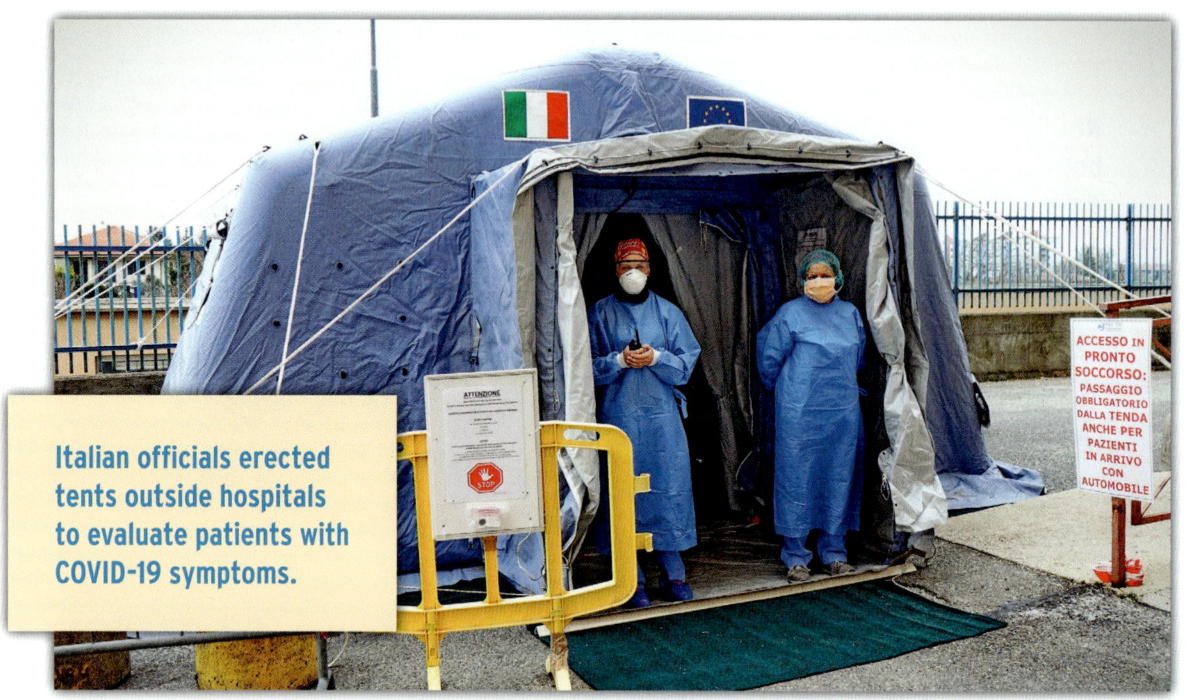

Italian officials erected tents outside hospitals to evaluate patients with COVID-19 symptoms.

first COVID-19 case in late February 2020. On March 9, the country enacted a national lockdown. Nonessential travel was prohibited, and many businesses had to close. Despite the lockdown, Italy had more than 100,000 confirmed cases and 12,000 deaths by the end of March. Hospitals in the country were overwhelmed with COVID-19 patients. Often, doctors had to choose which patients received life-saving care.

New York City

In the United States, New York City soon faced a similar outbreak. Between March and May 2020, the city had more than 200,000 confirmed COVID-19 cases. In late March, the city had implemented a stay-at-home order to try to keep the virus from spreading. People were asked to stay in their homes and travel only for essential reasons, such as buying groceries or seeking medical help. However, the stay-at-home order came too late. New York City hospitals were filled with COVID-19 patients throughout the spring. Doctors reported patients dying while waiting for intensive care unit (ICU) beds to become available. Hospital morgues soon became too full to store the bodies of deceased patients. So, bodies were stored in refrigerated trucks.

Public Health

As COVID-19 spread through the United States, public health officials focused on trying to slow the virus's spread. Although the CDC and HHS established pandemic safety guidelines, it was up

In several states, protesters demanded their governors lift stay-at-home orders and allow businesses to reopen.

to cities and states to implement and enforce precautions.

Many states passed mask mandates requiring people to wear face masks in public. Governors also closed schools, churches, gyms, and other public places. In late March and early April, many states passed stay-at-home orders. People were also encouraged to practice social distancing. This meant staying at least six feet (2 m) away from others in public.

Some states were reluctant to pass pandemic restrictions. State leaders argued such laws restricted personal freedom. North Dakota governor Doug Burgum, for example, resisted passing any pandemic restrictions until November 14. By then, North Dakota had the highest COVID-19 death rate of any state or country in the world. About 1 in 10 North Dakota citizens had COVID-19, and 1 in 1,000 had died from the disease.

Other states, such as Vermont, were quick to respond to the viral threat. The state introduced social distancing measures early in the pandemic. Vermont's government also partnered with motels to help reduce crowding in places such as retirement homes and homeless shelters, where individuals were more likely to catch the virus. These measures helped reduce viral spread statewide. In the beginning of 2021, Vermont had an infection rate of 1,654 cases per 100,000 people. North Dakota's infection rate was 12,610 cases per 100,000 people.

PIVOTAL PERSON: DR. ANTHONY FAUCI

Dr. Anthony Fauci was the director of the National Institute of Allergies and Infectious Diseases during the pandemic. He quickly emerged as a leading voice on fighting COVID-19. Fauci worked closely with US president Donald Trump as a member of the White House Coronavirus Task Force. Fauci often spoke publicly on behalf of the president to provide pandemic updates. He also encouraged safety measures, such as wearing masks and social distancing. Many Americans appreciated Fauci's clear communication about COVID-19. He was praised for his honesty and his efforts to promote factual precautions based on science.

Dr. Fauci addresses reporters at a COVID-19 update in January 2020.

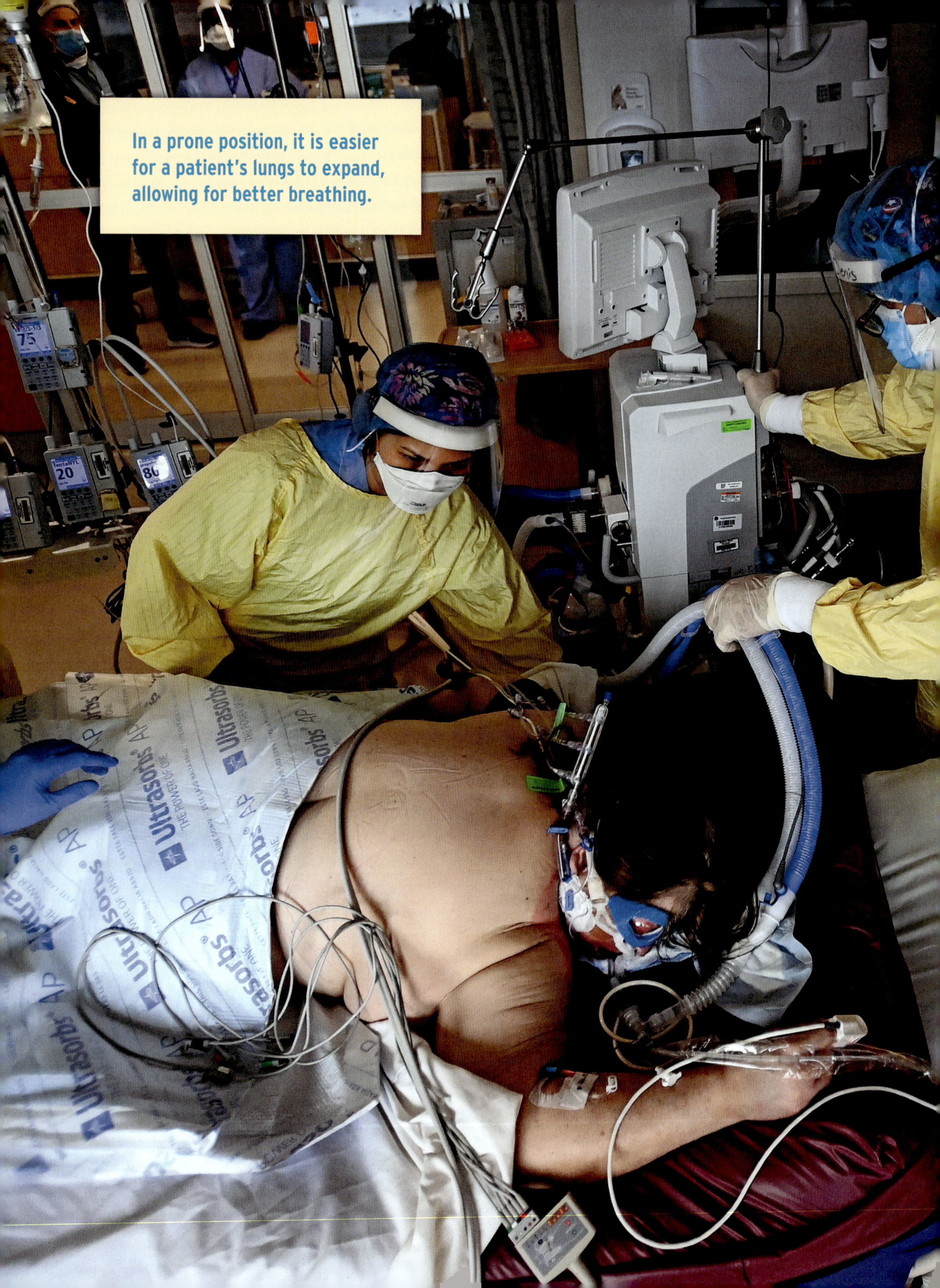

In a prone position, it is easier for a patient's lungs to expand, allowing for better breathing.

Chapter 6

ON THE FRONT LINES

No one was more affected by COVID-19's spread than frontline health-care workers. Doctors and nurses spent long days at crowded hospitals caring for COVID-19 patients. Some worked 13-hour shifts with few breaks.

Frontline workers faced serious challenges in treating patients. Early in the pandemic, there were no medications proven effective to treat COVID-19. So, doctors and nurses focused on treating symptoms, such as trouble breathing. For example, nurses found that putting patients on their stomachs for part of each day improved their breathing. This practice is called proning. However, it took up to six people to turn a patient over safely. On a busy hospital floor, it could be hard to find a team to do so.

Ventilators also helped patients struggling to breathe. These machines pump air into a patient's airways. Many hospitals did not have enough ventilators to treat COVID-19 patients.

President Trump was briefly hospitalized with COVID-19 in October. While there, he was treated with remdesivir.

So, some doctors had to hook multiple patients up to a single ventilator at once. This reduced the ventilator's effectiveness. It also increased the risk of spreading infections between patients.

In October, the US Food and Drug Administration (FDA) approved the antiviral drug remdesivir to treat COVID-19. Remdesivir prevented the virus from making copies of itself, improving a COVID-19 patient's chances of survival. However, it could not cure the illness.

Suiting Up

Doctors and nurses needed extensive personal protective equipment (PPE) to protect themselves from the virus. Typical PPE included scrubs, a protective suit, a medical gown, gloves, a face mask, a head covering, goggles, and a face shield. This PPE was often uncomfortable. Protective suits were hot. Goggles fogged up, making it difficult to see. Masks and goggles left cuts or bruises on wearers' noses and foreheads.

Many US hospitals faced PPE shortages during the pandemic. So, doctors and nurses were often forced to reuse masks and other PPE. This was dangerous. Most PPE is meant to be thrown away after one use. Reused PPE was not as safe or effective as fresh PPE.

To cope with PPE shortages, some medical workers made homemade masks and medical gowns. The Tennessee health department even suggested making masks out of diapers. It also suggested wearing swim goggles instead of medical goggles.

Many people accused the federal government of failing to address PPE shortages. Since 2003, the government had failed to maintain the SNS. So, much of its equipment was expired or

in low supply. States that requested PPE from the SNS did not receive enough. Many states tried to buy PPE directly from manufacturers. However, the high demand for PPE around the world meant that it was often expensive or hard to find.

In August 2020, dozens of nurses in Henderson, Nevada, protested PPE shortages.

More Shortages

Hospitals around the United States also ran out of ICU beds for COVID-19 patients. Many hospitals tried to create space by placing ICU beds in other sections of the hospital. Health officials also set up hospital tents in parking lots, event centers, and parks.

Hospitals typically treat patients in order of severity and then order of arrival. However, many hospitals were flooded with so many severely ill patients at one time that it was impossible to treat them all. On March 23, a group of doctors and scholars published guidelines in the *New England Journal of Medicine* to help determine which patients to treat first. They suggested prioritizing younger patients and those most likely to make a full recovery.

Even when hospitals had enough space, they struggled to keep enough staff. Before the pandemic, experts had predicted the United States would face a shortage of half a million nurses.

Older nurses were expected to retire without enough young nurses to replace them. During the pandemic, the shortage grew worse as health-care workers caught the virus and couldn't work.

An Impossible Job

Hospitals and health officials found different ways to address the nursing shortage. In November, North Dakota's governor issued an order allowing nurses with COVID-19 to work if they weren't experiencing symptoms. In many states, doctors and nurses moved to ICUs from other hospital departments. And, travel nurses went to states with major COVID-19 outbreaks to provide care. A travel nurse is hired by a hospital to fill a short-term staffing need. However, there were often not enough travel nurses to go around.

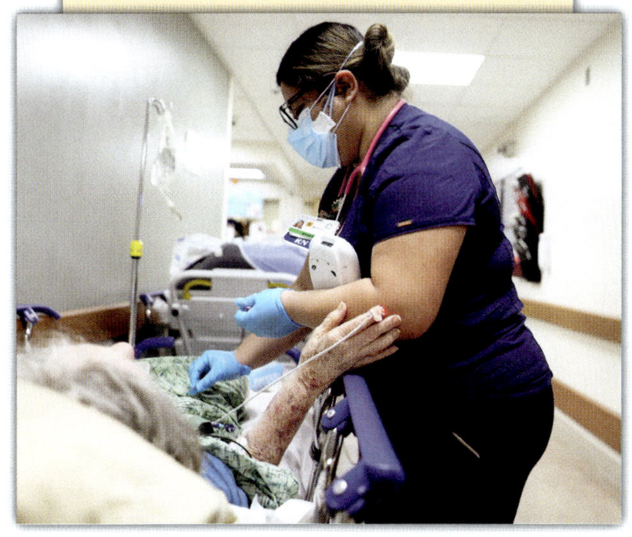

Some hospitals were forced to treat COVID-19 patients in hallways instead of hospital rooms.

Emotional and Physical Toll

By September 2020, at least 1,700 health-care workers had died of COVID-19 in the United States. A spring 2020 survey from the American Academy of Nurses found that 87 percent of nurses were afraid of going to work. Only 11 percent of the surveyed nurses felt prepared to care for

COVID-19 patients. Some doctors and nurses quit or were fired after they refused to work in unsafe conditions due to lack of PPE. The constant stress of caring for COVID-19 patients took a physical and emotional toll on health-care workers. Many were exhausted from working long hours. Medical workers also faced depression and anxiety after watching so many patients die. Many hospitals restricted visitors to prevent the virus from spreading. This meant medical workers were the only ones available to comfort dying patients whose families were not allowed to visit.

Even after their shifts ended, many health-care workers felt they could not fully relax. Even with PPE, medical workers risked catching the virus and spreading it to their families. Some health-care workers quarantined themselves in a room at home, away from their families. Others stayed in different homes altogether. Doctors and nurses could go weeks without seeing their loved ones.

Supporting Health-Care Heroes

Many everyday citizens stepped up to support health workers. Dental clinics, manufacturing companies, and factories donated extra PPE to hospitals in need. The organization Hospitality for Hope partnered with more than 17,000 hotels around the United States to donate empty hotel rooms to health-care workers. That way, workers otherwise unable to quarantine from their families had somewhere to stay. Medical students and other hospital staff

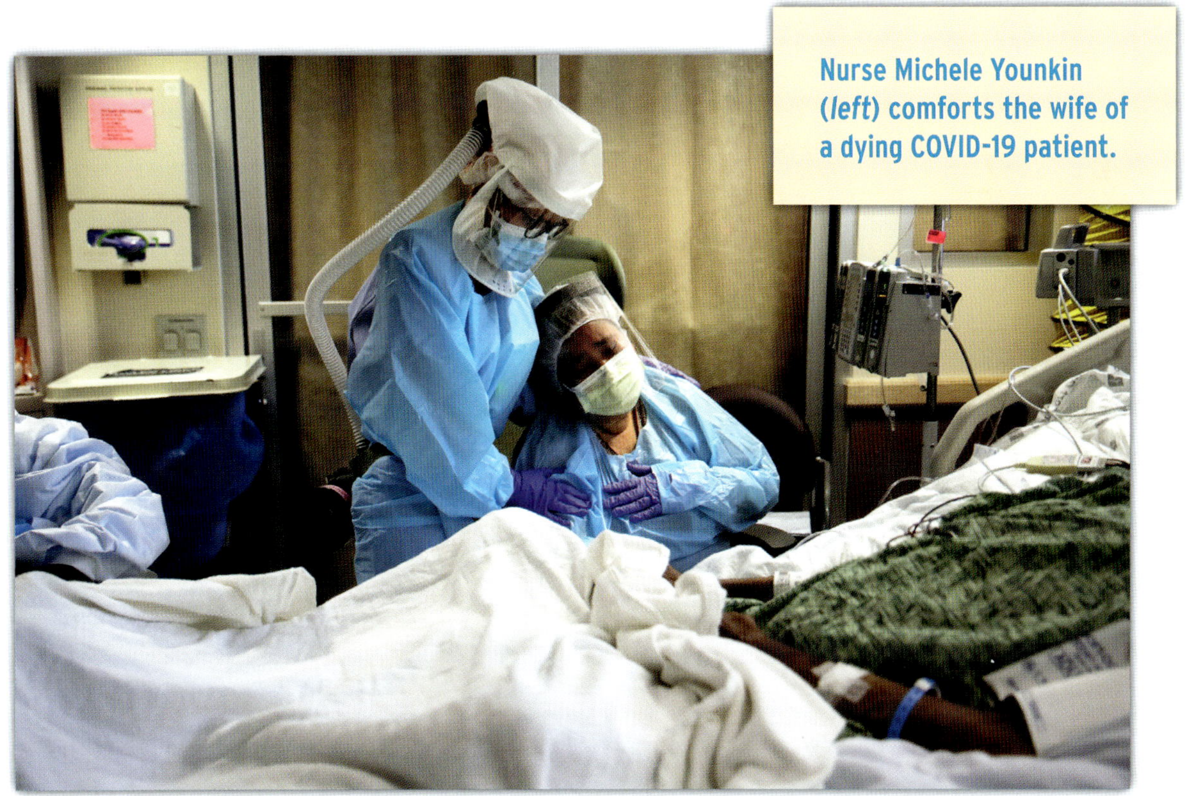

Nurse Michele Younkin (*left*) comforts the wife of a dying COVID-19 patient.

also provided childcare for busy doctors and nurses. And, many restaurants donated meals to feed hungry hospital workers.

Hope and Change

By early 2021, more than 21 million Americans had been infected with COVID-19, and an average of 1,100 people were dying each day. The United States had the highest case and death counts in the world. Still, health-care workers and everyday Americans had reason for hope. Since the start of the pandemic, doctors and nurses had developed more effective strategies to treat COVID-19 patients. So, fewer hospitalized patients died than in the pandemic's early days.

First responders in Mount Kisco, New York, applauded hospital workers during shift changes.

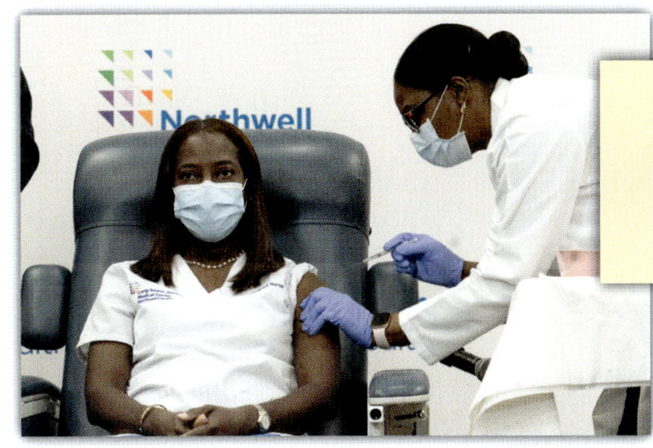

New York nurse Sandra Lindsay was the first American to receive Pfizer's COVID-19 vaccine after it was declared safe.

In December 2020, vaccines from drug companies Pfizer and Moderna had been authorized for use in the United States. The first doses were administered that month. Many went to frontline health workers. By April 2021, the United States was administering 2.8 million vaccine doses per day on average. Health experts estimated most US adults would be vaccinated by that summer. In the meantime, COVID-19 vaccines made people optimistic that the pandemic would soon be over. Doctors, nurses, and public health officials looked toward the future, hoping what they learned during the COVID-19 pandemic could help them in future pandemics.

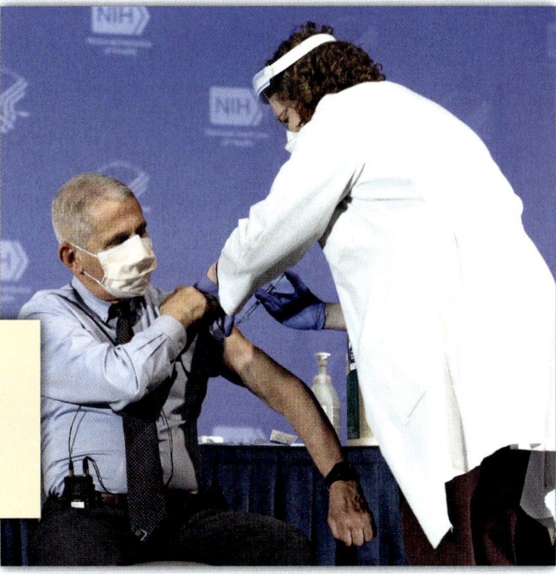

Dr. Anthony Fauci publicly received the Moderna vaccine to promote the vaccination effort.

TIMELINE

MARCH 1918
The first documented case of the 1918 influenza pandemic occurs, at Camp Funston in Kansas.

1918

1946
The Centers for Disease Control and Prevention (CDC) is founded in Atlanta, Georgia.

1946

1948
The World Health Organization (WHO) is founded.

1948

1919

1919
The 1918 influenza pandemic ends.

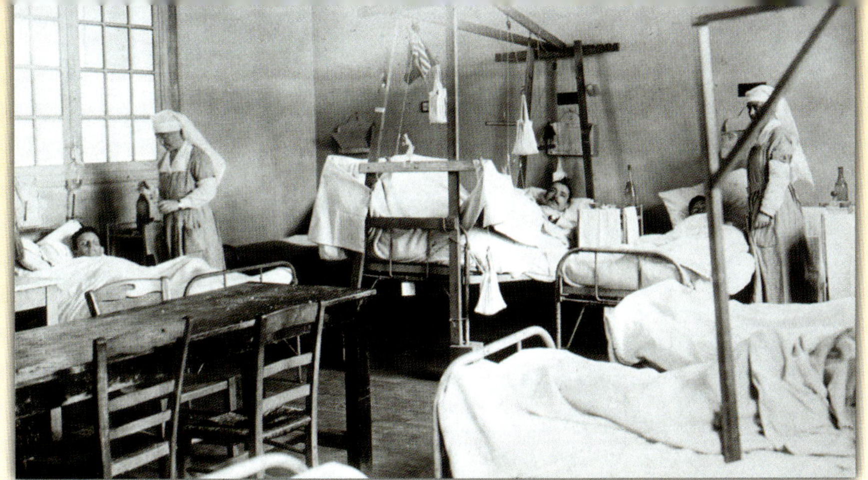

2003

An existing stockpile of medicines and vaccines is expanded to become the Strategic National Stockpile (SNS).

JANUARY 20, 2020

The United States reports its first COVID-19 case.

DECEMBER 2019

COVID-19 is first detected in Wuhan, China.

MARCH 11, 2020

The WHO declares COVID-19 a pandemic.

OCTOBER 2020

The US Food and Drug Administration (FDA) approves the drug remdesivir for treating COVID-19.

APRIL 2021

The United States is administering more than 2.8 million COVID-19 vaccine doses per day on average.

LATE MARCH–EARLY APRIL 2020

Many US governors pass stay-at-home orders.

SEPTEMBER 2020

At least 1,700 US health workers have died of COVID-19.

DECEMBER 2020

Vaccines from drug companies Pfizer and Moderna are authorized for use in the United States.

GLOSSARY

case fatality rate—the proportion of infected individuals who die from a disease.

Centers for Disease Control and Prevention (CDC)—the main national health organization in the United States. The CDC works to control the spread of disease and maintain and improve public health in the United States and other countries.

civilian—a person who is not an active member of the military.

depression—a state of feeling sad or dejected.

disinfect—to clean something so that it is free of germs.

droplet—a tiny drop of liquid.

epidemiologist—someone who studies how diseases spread.

hygiene—conditions or practices of cleanliness that are required for good health.

immune system—the system that protects the body from infection and disease. Someone who is immune to a disease is resistant to it.

intensive care unit (ICU)—a department of a hospital for very sick patients.

lockdown—a temporary measure ordered by government officials in which people are required to stay at home and limit public contact.

mandate—an official order.

morgue—a place where dead bodies are kept temporarily before being buried or cremated.

novel—new and different from what has previously been known.

outbreak—a sudden increase in the occurrence of illness.

quarantine—to separate from others in order to stop a disease from spreading.

racist—having the belief that one race is better than another.

respiratory—having to do with the system of organs involved with breathing.

sanitize—to make something free from disease by cleaning it.

segregated—separated from a larger group, especially by race.

shortage—a lack of something that is needed.

stockpile—a reserve of something that has been built up over time.

ventilation—the process of allowing fresh air to enter and move through. An area with good ventilation is ventilated.

World Health Organization (WHO)—an agency of the United Nations that works to maintain and improve the health of people around the world.

World War I—from 1914 to 1918, fought in Europe. Great Britain, France, Russia, the United States, and their allies were on one side. Germany, Austria-Hungary, and their allies were on the other side.

Booklinks
NONFICTION NETWORK
FREE! ONLINE NONFICTION RESOURCES

To learn more about medical mobilization, please visit **abdobooklinks.com** or scan this QR code. These links are routinely monitored and updated to provide the most current information available.

INDEX